# ISLANDS

Written by Ben Lerwill
Illustrated by Li Zhang

WELBECK
EDITIONS

Published in 2022 by Welbeck Editions

An imprint of Welbeck Children's Limited,
part of Welbeck Publishing Group.
Based in London and Sydney.
www.welbeckpublishing.com

ISBN 978 1 91351 922 3

Printed in Heshan, China

10 9 8 7 6 5 4 3 2 1

# CONTENTS

# Surrounded by Water

An island is an area of land that is completely surrounded by water and smaller than a continent. Islands come in countless shapes and sizes. Some are home to millions of people, others have almost no life at all. Some are covered in thick jungle, others are coated in ice. Some are millions of years old ... and others are younger than you!

This amazing variety is what makes islands so special. But what are they exactly? And how were they formed? Well, no matter how big or small they are, and no matter where on the planet they're found, most islands can be described as either volcanic or continental.

## Volcanic islands

A volcanic island, also known as an oceanic island, is made when an underwater volcano explodes on the ocean floor, forcing out so much lava that it eventually reaches above the waves. When the lava cools and becomes solid, land is formed. Islands like this can still appear today!

We can also find other types of island around the world:

**Coral islands** are formed from the bodies of millions of corals, which are small sea animals found in warm sea waters.

**Barrier islands** lie next to a coastline. They're usually long and narrow, and made of sand. They can help to protect the coast from storms.

**Tidal islands** are areas of land that are cut off from the mainland whenever the tide is high. When the tide's low, they're not islands anymore!

**Artificial islands** are built by people, rather than nature. Islands like this are usually made as somewhere to live, or to visit.

**Coral island**

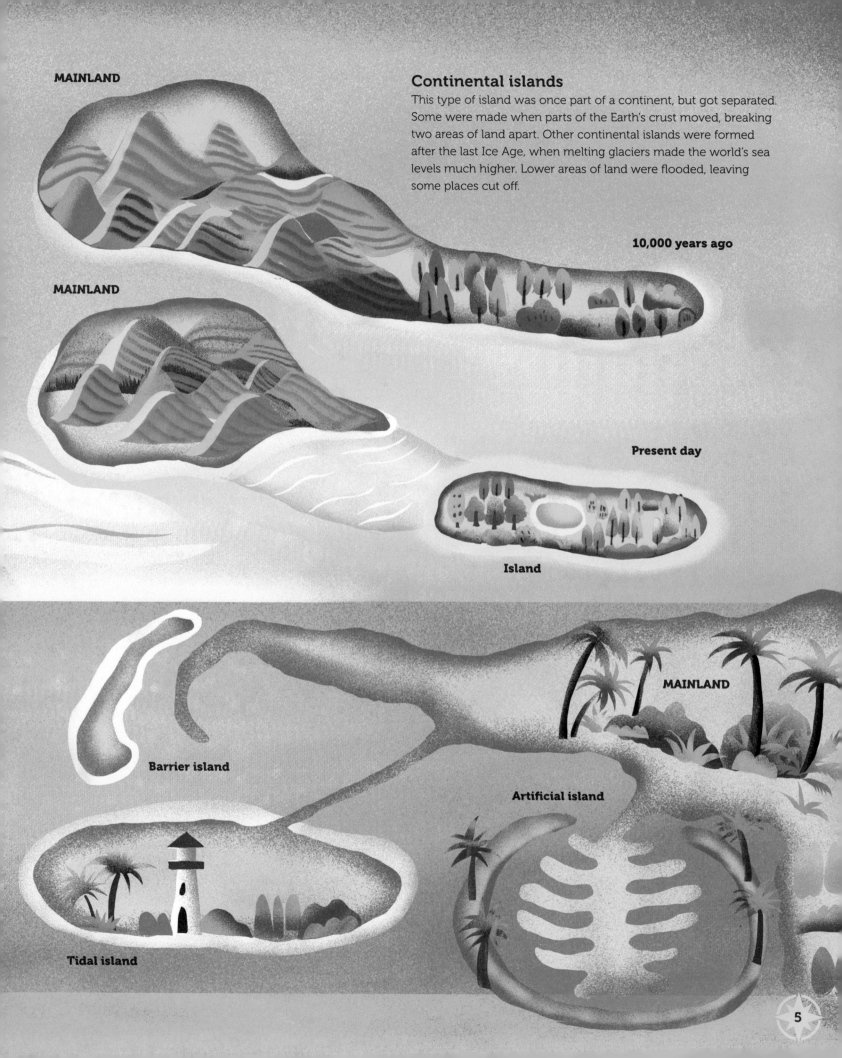

**MAINLAND**

## Continental islands
This type of island was once part of a continent, but got separated. Some were made when parts of the Earth's crust moved, breaking two areas of land apart. Other continental islands were formed after the last Ice Age, when melting glaciers made the world's sea levels much higher. Lower areas of land were flooded, leaving some places cut off.

**10,000 years ago**

**MAINLAND**

**Present day**

**Island**

**Barrier island**

**MAINLAND**

**Artificial island**

**Tidal island**

# Island Wildlife

From mysterious mammals to rare reptiles, island wildlife can be truly fascinating. But why? On a huge continent, animals that can't swim or fly can still move from place to place quite easily, but that's not true with islands. Island animals often have no choice but to adapt to the habitat they live in.

For an animal on a remote island, there might be fewer predators for it to avoid, and only certain foods for it to eat. This means that animals on islands often evolve (change over time) in different ways than animals elsewhere. Because of this, many islands are home to very unusual creatures. All this is true when talking about plants, too.

Many species of animal and plant are endemic to one island, which means they're found nowhere else in the world. Lemurs, for example, live only on the island of Madagascar. They thrive because there are no other apes or monkeys there.

The wildlife of an island has often been there for thousands or even millions of years, so it can damage the balance of nature if new plants or animals are introduced.

## How do animals and plants get to islands in the first place?

A continental island often has similar wildlife to the land it was once joined to. In other words, these creatures have been there ever since the island was formed. But there are other ways that animals and plants have arrived on islands, too.

Birds, bats, and even some insects can fly across the sea to reach an island. Sometimes very strong winds can blow them there.

Branches, trees, and big clumps of soil can sometimes be washed out to sea with animals and insects on them. Some of these can float away and reach islands.

Plant seeds can float for long distances and sometimes wash up on islands, where they grow.

Some species of plants and animals were brought to islands on purpose, by humans. This might have been as pets, as farm animals, or because people thought it would be good for the island.

Ships have sometimes brought animals to islands by accident. For example, the wild mice on board a ship might run ashore and never return.

# Humans and Islands

Not all islands are wild places. Many have villages, towns, and cities. You might even live on an island yourself! Great Britain, Japan, Barbados, and New Zealand are all examples of island countries—and people also live on thousands of much smaller islands around the world.

Today the whole world is well connected, but in the past some islands were very isolated. This meant that they often had their own special ways of living, learning, cooking, relaxing, and celebrating. Many islands still keep their traditions alive. On the Pacific island of Niue, for example, many boys don't have their hair cut until they become teenagers!

Islands often have very interesting histories. Some islands have had people living on them since prehistoric times, while others have been visited by explorers, castaways, pirates, and invaders.

Climate change is a big problem for some low-lying islands, because of rising sea levels. In places like the Maldives, a chain of islands in the Indian Ocean, there's a danger that people's homes might be swamped by seawater if things don't change.

# Island record-breakers

**Ì** is the name for the island of Iona in the Scottish Gaelic language. No other island in the world has such a short name.

**Luzon** in the Philippines has more unique mammals than any other island. Giant fruit bats, long-nosed forest mice, and rare warty pigs all live here.

**Bishop Rock** in the Isles of Scilly is the world's smallest island with a building on it. It has one lighthouse—and that's it!

**Greenland** is the biggest island in the world. It's more than twice the size of the world's second biggest island.

**Sweden** is the country with the most islands. It has more than 265,000—although only around 1,000 of them have people on them.

**Ilha da Queimada Grande** in Brazil is the most dangerous island in the world. It has so many poisonous snakes that humans aren't allowed there!

**Tristan da Cunha** in the Atlantic Ocean is the most remote group of islands in the world. It takes six days to sail there from the nearest country.

**Java** in Indonesia is the island with the most people. More than 140 million people live here!

## Dolphins and dingoes

Fraser Island is an amazing place for wildlife. Monitor lizards wander the forests, tawny frogmouths swoop through the trees, and rare humpback dolphins swim offshore. It's also home to packs of golden-coated wild dogs called dingoes. These cunning canines are at the top of the Fraser Island food chain. Pet dogs are banned here because dingoes can be dangerous. Don't try to stroke them!

## Fraser Island – or K'gari?

People have been living in Australia for 50,000 years. Today, some Australians still have family connections to ancestors who lived here many thousands of years ago. We describe these Australians as indigenous, or native. Indigenous people have their own beautiful name for Fraser Island: they call it *K'gari*, meaning "paradise." In indigenous culture, *K'gari* was the name of a goddess who fell to Earth, loved what she found, and never wanted to leave.

# Fraser Island
## Australia

If you run your finger along a map of Australia's sunny east coast, you'll find an island with a difference. Fraser Island has towering rainforest, clear lakes and incredible wildlife, but what really makes it unusual is that it's the world's largest sand island. Instead of being made of rocks, most of the island is made of sand. Even its main road is also a beach! Can you imagine a sandcastle the size of a city? That's Fraser Island!

### Beach wreck

Halfway along the island's longest beach is a very strange sight: the rusting skeleton of an old passenger ship. This is all that remains of SS *Maheno*, which used to sail between Australia and New Zealand. It was a very stylish ship, with a dining room and a grand piano, but in 1935 it washed up on the beach in a storm. The shipwreck has been here ever since.

### A story of sand

Fraser Island was formed by two of nature's best builders: the wind and the waves! For the past two million years, sand has slowly been swept away from Australia's beaches and out into the ocean. Fraser Island was once just a low shelf of land, but over time, the sand being carried by the waves got stuck here, and stayed. The island grew, and grew, and grew. Today it's as long as a motorway, as tall as a skyscraper, and full of giant dunes and thick forests.

# Île de la Cité
## Paris, France

Like a delicious pan of food, Paris bubbles with different flavors. France's capital city is a place of art and music, cafés and bakeries, cobbled avenues and mazy markets. It is big, busy, and brimming with noise. But it wasn't always like this. It began life as a small village on an island in the middle of the River Seine, and the island is still there, right in the heart of it all. Welcome to Île de la Cité.

### One island, many bridges

Île de la Cité might be an island, but you don't need to sail there—or swim! On both sides of the island there are bridges connecting it to the rest of the city, and it's easy to stroll across. The most famous bridge is the handsome Pont Neuf. Its name means "New Bridge," although it's now more than 400 years old!

## Notre-Dame

This soaring, twin-towered cathedral is one of the country's most important buildings. It took more than 180 years to build, and powerful kings and emperors have been crowned inside. One of the most famous French books of all time, *The Hunchback of Notre-Dame*, is set right here. There's even a Disney film that tells the same story.

Disaster struck Notre-Dame in 2019 when a raging fire destroyed large parts of the cathedral. Tens of thousands of bees were living in hives on the roof—but astonishingly, they survived!

## Rainbow glass

Today, the Île de la Cité is always very busy with visitors. Many of them also come to see Sainte-Chapelle, an 800-year-old chapel filled with rainbow-colored stained-glass windows. Can you think of any other famous Paris landmarks?

The building style of Notre-Dame is known as gothic architecture. The stone structures that look like giraffe necks are called flying buttresses, and they support the main walls.

## Volcanic islands

When you stare up at the steep slopes and jagged rocks of St. Kilda, what you're seeing is part of the rim of an ancient volcano. The volcano was active about 65 million years ago, not long after dinosaurs were roaming the Earth! Most of it has now crumbled into the ocean, but St. Kilda has been left with some of the highest sea cliffs in Europe.

## Special seabirds

St. Kilda is a magnet for seabirds. Every year, hundreds of thousands of puffins, gannets, and fulmars come here to breed. They make for an unforgettable sight. The bright-beaked puffins waddle around outside their burrows, the gannets arrow into the sea to catch fish, and the fulmars soar on straight wings like fighter planes. Other seabirds, like guillemots and skuas, also come to St. Kilda.

# St. Kilda
## Scotland

Way out in the North Atlantic Ocean, where the waves are wild and the winds are fierce, you'll find spectacular St. Kilda. It might be a part of Scotland, but this remote archipelago (or group of islands) is a long way from anywhere. No one lives here any-more, and the nearest port is several hours away by boat. The good news is that this means wildlife can thrive—every spring and summer, the enormous cliffs here are home to a million seabirds!

## At home in the ocean

You might think a lump of volcanic rock in the middle of the ocean would be a strange place to live—and you'd be right! But for around 2,000 years, people did live on St. Kilda. They built stone houses, hunted seabirds and worked hard to grow crops. But the weather was harsh and life was difficult. In 1930, the people who lived here moved away forever.

## The islands

St. Kilda is made up of four main islands. Dùn, Soay, and Boreray are the smaller ones and Hirta is the biggest, with the highest sea cliffs in all of the UK.

## Wonderful wildlife

Seabirds aren't the only animals found here. Wild Soay sheep with brown coats and long horns live on the islands, and gray seals are sometimes seen on the rocks. St. Kilda even has its own kind of field mouse, which is much larger than those from the mainland and isn't found anywhere else in the world.

# Snow Hill Island
## Antarctica

Picture a land of ice, snow, and freezing winds, where penguins, seals, and whales swim in the chilly seas. A place so remote that only a few lucky people have ever stepped foot on its shores. This is Antarctica, the great white continent at the bottom of the world map. The winter temperatures here plummet lower than anywhere else on Earth. And just off the coastline, glistening in the frosty southern light, you'll find Snow Hill Island.

### An island under snow

The island is usually surrounded by ice, so only special ships—called icebreakers—can even get close. It's also almost completely covered in snow. Underneath this white crust, however, the island is made from the kind of ancient, fossil-rich rocks that we find in many other parts of the world. Hundreds of millions of years ago, all of Antarctica was part of a huge supercontinent called Gondwana, connected to places like Africa and Australia!

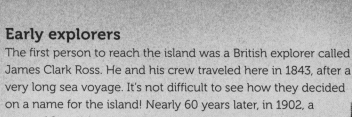

## Early explorers

The first person to reach the island was a British explorer called James Clark Ross. He and his crew traveled here in 1843, after a very long sea voyage. It's not difficult to see how they decided on a name for the island! Nearly 60 years later, in 1902, a team of Swedish scientists arrived and built a small wooden hut, named after Otto Nordenskjöld, whose team built it. Today, it is the oldest building in Antarctica.

## Penguin royalty

The seas around the island are usually frozen solid with ice. This is the ideal environment for emperor penguins, the largest penguin species in the world. A colony of these incredible flightless birds breeds here every winter. The mothers and fathers are both excellent parents, working as a team to make sure their chicks are kept safe. Emperor penguins sometimes slide around on their tummies—but when they stand up, they're as tall as a six-year-old child!

## A special land

Antarctica and its islands are not part of any country. They have no government—and apart from a few scientists and other staff, they have no human population either. The whole continent is protected as a scientific preserve.

## Plans and problems

Palm Jumeirah was controversial when it was built because it had such a big impact on fish and other underwater life. Lots of coral was killed and destroyed. Because of the shape of the island, it also made it much more difficult for water to flow normally.

## A world of islands

Palm Jumeirah isn't the only manmade island in Dubai—there's even another one shaped like a palm tree! But maybe the strangest of all is The World, made up of hundreds of small sand islands that have been shaped to look like the world map.

# Palm Jumeirah
## United Arab Emirates

This unusual group of islands sits under the sweltering desert sun of western Asia. When you look at it from above, you can see it's almost perfectly symmetrical—and shaped just like a palm tree! This is because it's manmade. Before the year 2001, there was nothing here but seawater and sand. Then a huge team of builders and divers brought in sand, dredged from the sea floor, and millions of tons of rocks, blasted out of a nearby mountain range, to construct the islands that we see today.

Millions of real palm trees grow in the United Arab Emirates. They produce soft, sugary fruits called dates. The trees grow well in hot countries.

### A walk in the park

The island is crammed full of towers and buildings, but there's greenery too. Al Ittihad Park has long gardens filled with over 60 kinds of local trees and plants. Dozens of bird species have been spotted here, including doves, parakeets, and sunbirds.

### Ride the rails

The trunk of the palm tree is also the main road for people driving onto the island, and all 16 of the fronds, or branches, have their own roads too. There's even a monorail that zooms right the way up the trunk to the very tip of the tree. The final stop is a giant hotel with more than 1,500 rooms, a huge water park, and an enormous aquarium.

### Palm life

The Palm Jumeirah has offices, restaurants, shops, mansions, and apartments. Some people live here all year round. What do you think it would be like to have a home on an island like this?

# Easter Island
## Chile

Mystery hangs over Easter Island. This hilly green landmass, washed by winter rain and bashed by the stormy waves of the Pacific, stands all alone in the middle of the ocean. But despite being one of the most isolated places on Earth, the island is dotted with around 1,000 giant statues, their long stone faces gazing inland. Why are they here? And who made them?

### One island, two names

For the settlers who first lived here, the island had the same name that they did: Rapa Nui. But today, although some people still call the island Rapa Nui, others call it Easter Island. Why? Way back in 1722, a Dutch explorer sailed to the island. He arrived on Easter Sunday, so he gave it a new title—and the name stuck.

### A home in the ocean

Historians think that people first came to live on the island more than 800 years ago. These people are known as the Rapa Nui, and they would have come here in wooden canoes. Can you imagine arriving at this tiny speck in the ocean, more than 1,250 miles from the nearest island? We can only guess at how the Rapa Nui found their way here, but we know they must have been excellent survivors—their descendants still live on the island today.

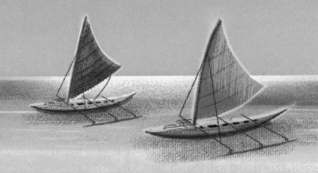

### Magical moai

Easter Island's famous statues are known as *moai* (pronounced "mo-why"). They're carved from blocks of the island's dark volcanic rock, and experts think most of them were made between 350 and 950 years ago using stone tools. Some of them are as high as a house and can weigh as much as ten elephants! The *moai* were probably created to remember important Rapa Nui people who had died, but no one knows exactly how the huge, heavy statues were moved into place.

### Enjoying the island

People from around the world travel to Easter Island to see the *moai*, but the statues are just one reason to come here. Some visitors ride horses across the hills to enjoy the quietest parts of the island, while divers and snorkelers explore the waters offshore, which are full of fascinating species like trumpetfish and porcupinefish.

# Surtsey
## Iceland

Surtsey is a serious surprise. When you see this volcanic island's steep slopes and sea-bashed shoreline, you might think you're looking at somewhere ancient. In fact, it didn't exist at all until the 1960s! Formed by an underwater eruption off the coast of Iceland, this remarkable island is even younger than inventions like the television and the telephone. Up until a few short decades ago, there was nothing to see here but sea!

### Bursting to life

It was November 1963 when an unexpected rumble under the sea led to the eruption that brought Surtsey to life. Columns of dark smoke and streams of fiery lava soon started appearing above the waves. Islands made by underwater volcanoes usually get washed away by the sea, but so much lava was produced here that the rocks of Surtsey hardened and became a permanent island. The people of Iceland were astonished—and their country needed a brand-new map!

Only scientists are allowed to land on Surtsey. Tourists have to stay on boats and look from a distance. This is so that humans don't change the island in any way.

## Down in the south

Surtsey is the southernmost point of Iceland—but it's definitely not the only part of the country formed by a volcano! Iceland sits on something called the Mid-Atlantic Ridge, which is where two enormous pieces of the world meet each other, a bit like a line in a giant jigsaw puzzle. These pieces of the world—known as tectonic plates—rub against each other, which can cause earthquakes and big eruptions. In 2010, a volcano erupted in Iceland that filled the air with so much ash that planes all across Europe needed to stay on the ground for six days.

## A new home

One of the most incredible parts of Surtsey's story is how the island has become a home for different plants and animals. Scientists think that seeds must have been carried here by ocean currents, because within a few years there were mosses, fungi, and leafy plants growing on the island. These helped to attract insects and birds, and today Surtsey has wildlife that includes seals, beetles, and almost 90 species of bird.

## An uncertain future

Surtsey is an amazing place, but experts agree that it won't be with us forever. The island is slowly being eroded, or chipped away, by the sea. By 2100, most of it, apart from its tough core, will probably have disappeared.

## Liberty lady

A short distance away, on Liberty Island, stands the world-famous Statue of Liberty. It is a symbol of freedom and opportunity. The torch-bearing statue was a gift from France and has been here since 1885.

## The early days

Hundreds of years ago, the island was silent and sandy. Local boats would come here to catch shellfish and other seafood. Later it became a place of punishment, where pirates were hanged. Then in 1774 a small tavern was opened, serving drinks and food to fishermen—the man who opened it was named Samuel Ellis, and the island still bears his name.

## Immigrant island

Two centuries ago, large numbers of people started sailing to New York City, looking for a new home and a better life. Many of them had crossed the Atlantic Ocean from Europe. By the 1890s, so many immigrants were coming here every year that the city needed somewhere to register them all when they arrived. Ellis Island was the answer.

## New arrivals

A building known as an immigration station was built on the island. It was ready to use on 1 January 1892. When people arrived, usually after a very long sea voyage, they had to be interviewed by officials and checked by doctors. For millions of immigrants, Ellis Island was their very first experience of America. Today, experts think that 40 percent of the country's population has an ancestor that passed through the buildings here!

# Ellis Island
## USA

This is a tiny island with a super-sized history. Ellis Island sits in New York Harbor, just a short boat ride from the bright lights and busy avenues of New York City, one of the biggest and busiest cities in the world. But little Ellis Island has many stories of its own: between 1892 and 1954, around 12 million people passed through the buildings here, arriving into the USA to start a new life.

### First in line

The very first immigrant to be checked and interviewed on Ellis Island was an Irish teenager named Annie Moore, who arrived in New York in 1892 with her two younger brothers. Their life in Ireland had been very hard. Because she was the first person in line, Annie was presented with a special gold ten-dollar coin.

# Miyajima
# Japan

There's an air of magic on Miyajima. This Japanese island, also known as Itsukushima, has been a holy place for local people for more than a thousand years. If you're lucky enough to visit, you'll find ancient temples, a sacred mountain, and one of the most precious shrines, or holy sites, in the country. The island is also home to a very special group of animals: hundreds of tame deer!

## Relax at a ryokan

Like many places in Japan, Miyajima has lots of small traditional hotels called *ryokans*. Their rooms are very bare but very comfortable, with special soft matting, and beds that lie right on the floor. Guests have to take their shoes off when they arrive, then use slippers. Most *ryokans* also have their own bath area, called an onsen, where guests can soak together in hot water.

## Deer oh deer

For centuries, the gentle Sika deer who live here were worshiped as messengers of the gods. Today people don't think of them in quite the same way, but the deer are still free to wander the streets and the seafront, where their soft spotted coats are a familiar sight. Sika deer are herbivores and like eating grass, leaves, and twigs, but be careful—if you're carrying food with you, you might find a wet nose seeking it out!

## Climbing the heights

The highest point of Miyajima is the sacred Mount Misen. Firs, red pines, and other trees grow on its slopes, and three different hiking trails lead all the way to the top. From the summit, the views stretch out right across the bay. But people aren't the only ones who make it this far—wild monkeys live up here too!

## Floating gate

Miyajima is famous around Japan for the bright red *torii* gate at the Itsukushima-jinja Shrine. Gates like this are found at shrines around the country, and for followers of the Shinto religion they represent a doorway between the earthly world and the holy world. Miyajima's giant *torii* gate was built in the 12th century right on the edge of the sea, so when the tide comes in it looks like it's floating.

## A mighty explosion

Around 3,500 years ago, Santoríni was the site of one of the largest volcanic eruptions ever seen. Smoke and ash filled the skies and red-hot lava spewed from the earth. The explosion was so big that some of the ash blew all the way to Egypt— 435 miles away! When you look at Santoríni today, what you're seeing is one half of the exploded volcano.

## Precious pumice

Santoríni has become one of the most popular holiday islands in Europe, with lots of hotels and beaches. So many, in fact, that some people worry there are too many tourists. But for a long time, the island made its money in a very different way: by selling huge amounts of pumice, a kind of rough volcanic rock which is easy to find here. Pumice contains lots of tiny "bubbles," or air pockets. This makes it very light, and people around the world still use it to rub dry skin from the bottom of their feet!

## Churches and donkeys

Some people like to say that Santorini has more churches than houses, and more donkeys than people! This isn't quite true, but the island is a very religious one, and has more than 600 churches and temples. Some of them are tiny! There are also many donkeys here. Tourists sometimes pay to ride them up Santorini's steep steps, but this can make the animals hot and tired. If you choose to walk rather than ride, it's better for your fitness— and much easier for the donkeys!

# Santorini
## Greece

The islands of Greece are scattered like jewels across the Aegean Sea. Some of these islands are just empty rocks, gleaming in the sunshine, but others are much bigger. One of the most famous is the dazzling, crescent-shaped island of Santorini, where walls of rock tower above the waves and pretty white buildings cluster on the clifftops. It looks lovely on holiday postcards... but it has a history full of fire and thunder.

### Tasty treat
Santorini has some special foods, including *tomatokeftedes*. These hot, crunchy snacks are made from fresh local tomatoes, feta cheese, and herbs that have been crushed, then fried in oil. Yum!

Santorini curves around a deep blue bay full of smaller islands. These were also part of the volcano—one of them, Nea Kameni, still has smoking craters!

## Nature running wild

Socotra is often described as the most alien-looking place on Earth, because the island has so many unusual plants, animals, and landscapes. The granite mountains are jagged and the sand dunes are huge. The dark and magical Hoq Cave, meanwhile, measures more than 25 football fields end to end!

## A cultural crossroads

Socotra has no written history, so its past is a bit of a mystery. What we do know is that different people have lived and traveled here for thousands of years. Egyptians, Greeks, and Romans all came to Socotra in search of precious things like frankincense, and the sap from dragon blood trees. Today the towns and villages on the island have a mix of cultural influences from Asia, Africa, and Europe. Many of the people who live here speak an ancient dialect called Soqotri—a language with no official written version!

## On the edge of the map

Sunny islands like this are often busy with holidaymakers and beach resorts. Not Socotra! Just one airplane lands here every week. The few travelers who come here are looking for nature and adventure. The island belongs to the country of Yemen, which is 185 miles away.

# Socotra
## Yemen

Imagine an island where the sands stretch out forever and the trees look like giant mushrooms. An island surrounded by clear blue waters, where dolphins swim and rare birds skim the waves. An island that looks like something from a dream. This distant land is one of the world's great travel secrets: a place which is thrilling to explore but tough to reach, hidden away where the Indian Ocean meets the Arabian Sea. Its name? Socotra.

## Dragon blood trees

Socotra is famous for its amazing dragon blood trees, which are tall and wide with a crown of thick, tangled branches. They take their name from the dark red sap they produce. Some people use this sap as a kind of medicine. Because Socotra is so isolated, these trees and many of the island's other strange plants are endemic—which means they're not found anywhere else on the planet!

## Made from nature

The islands are made from totora reeds: a tall, strong water plant that grows only in South America. Making an island from these reeds takes a lot of work. First, big blocks of earth and roots are cut from the lakebed and tied together, a bit like a giant raft. Then hundreds of armfuls of dried reeds are laid on top to make the islands comfortable and secure—some are big enough for six or seven families to live alongside each other.

## Sacred lake

Lake Titicaca has always been an important place, and not just for the Uros people. The Incas were a powerful group of people who ruled the area 500 years ago. They believed that the lake was the birthplace of the sun, where the whole world began.

The Uros people also use reeds to build their houses, and when the children go to school they even travel in boats made from reeds! Some islands have solar panels, which turn sunlight into electricity for the houses.

## Uros people

The handmade islands are the work of the Uros people, who have been living in this area for many centuries. Known for their fishing skills and colorful skirts, they first decided to build floating islands hundreds of years ago, as a way of staying safe from the Inca people, who were sometimes violent. Today, the remaining Uros people still live on more than 100 floating islands, on the Peru side of the lake.

# Uros Floating Islands
## Peru

Way up in the mountains of South America you'll find some remarkable manmade islands. They lie on Lake Titicaca, one of the highest lakes in the world. The lake is a beautiful place of age-old temples and mirror-calm waters, with its western shore in Peru and its eastern shore in Bolivia. Sitting on its surface, meanwhile, are some very special structures made from plants that grow in the water. These are the incredible Uros floating islands.

Many tourists come here to see the islands, and to meet the people living here. This creates a tricky situation: the Uros people earn money from these visitors, but it's hard for them to keep their old way of life.

# Galápagos Islands
## Ecuador

When the famous naturalist Charles Darwin sailed into the Galápagos Islands on the HMS *Beagle*, in 1835, his bushy whiskers must have trembled in amazement. These incredible islands are thronged with thousands of fascinating animals and plants, almost all of which can't be found anywhere else. Darwin described it as "a little world within itself," and almost 200 years later the Galápagos Islands remain one of the most precious places on the planet.

## Out in the Pacific

Welcome to a distant world of sandy beaches, high cliffs, and volcanic mountains. The 19 rugged islands of the Galápagos are hidden away in the South Pacific, far from any other land. Officially they belong to the country of Ecuador, in South America, which sits around three days away by boat.

## Slow and steady

Of all the animals that live here, the best known is the Galápagos giant tortoise. This remarkable reptile can live to over 100 years old and it spends almost 16 hours a day resting. When it's fully grown, it can weigh the same as ten schoolchildren! People think giant tortoises have been living here for around three million years.

## Theory of evolution

Giant tortoises were one of the animals that intrigued Charles Darwin when he arrived here. He noticed that tortoises on different islands had different types of shell. This, and other similar discoveries, inspired him to write a book called *On the Origin of Species*, which transformed how people thought about life on Earth. It talked about evolution, which is how humans and animals have changed to adapt to their surroundings since the start of time.

## Wild islands

One of the things that makes the wildlife here so extraordinary is its diversity. Sharp-beaked finches flitter between cactus flowers, marine iguanas crawl over salty rocks, and dark-feathered hawks soar above clifftops. The islands also have 486 different species of beetle!

## The HMS *Beagle*

Darwin's visit to the Galápagos was part of a five-year voyage on the HMS *Beagle*, a huge wooden sailing ship launched in London. The aim of the journey was to survey the coastline of South America—but new discoveries about the natural world were an added bonus. The 74 people on board included sailors, scientists, and other experts. They traveled right around the globe!

## Finding food

Pitcairn is too small to have an airport, so all its supplies arrive by sea. Because of this, the islanders try to grow whatever food they can. Sweet potatoes, bananas, sugarcane, and oranges all grow here—and there are beehives, too.

## Island life

After reaching the empty island, the sailors and the Tahitian women made basic houses and planted fruits and vegetables. They burned the ship, signaling they were here to stay. Within a few years, babies began to be born. Today, around 50 people still live on Pitcairn, and many of them can trace their family trees all the way back to the arrival of the HMS *Bounty*.

## Local language

Many islanders still speak a language called Pitkern, which is a mix between English and Tahitian. In Pitkern, "whata way ye?" means "how are you?" and "ye like-a sum whettles?" means "would you like something to eat?".

# Pitcairn Island
## Pacific Ocean

Finding Pitcairn Island on the world map isn't easy—but its strange story comes to life when you do. A little lump of volcanic green surrounded by the endless blue of the Pacific, the island is far-flung, fertile and full of history. More than 230 years ago, a small group of British sailors and Pacific Islanders arrived on its empty shores to start a new life ... and their descendants still live here today.

## Mutiny on the Bounty

Sometimes, real life can feel like a storybook. This was the case in 1789, when a British ship named HMS *Bounty* left the Pacific island of Tahiti to sail to the Caribbean, but there was trouble ahead. Some of the sailors became so unhappy with the ship's strict captain that they pushed him into a small boat with some of his helpers, then set them adrift! When sailors overthrow their captain like this, we call it a mutiny.

## On to Pitcairn

The sailors had decided they wanted to live on a sunny Pacific island. After the mutiny, they turned the HMS *Bounty* back to Tahiti, where they forced six men and 12 local women to join them. The selfish crew then sailed out into the ocean, looking for an island to be their new home. When they spotted Pitcairn through their telescopes, in January 1790, they decided to stay.

# Wrangel Island
## Russia

Polar bears padding along the shores. Musk oxen roaming the plains. Arctic foxes darting across the slopes. This ice-cold Russian island is one of the northernmost places on the planet—a little-known land of hulking mountains, lonely beaches, and endless valleys—but its isolated plains are a haven for animals. You can often count the number of people here on one hand, but there are always wild things on the move ...

### Bigfoot bears

The island has been a protected nature reserve since 1976, which is good news for the many creatures found here. Mammals such as musk oxen and reindeer wander through the wilderness, as do majestic, white-coated polar bears. These super-strong hunters walk across the frozen seas to reach Wrangel each year, where they raise their cubs. Adult bears have huge paws that act like snowshoes to spread their weight.

### Water world

Wrangel's amazing wildlife isn't just found on land. The seas here are alive with slow-swimming whales and big, blubbery walruses. Hungry bears sometimes prowl the beaches, waiting for walruses to come close enough to shore to be pounced upon. Can you imagine what a fearsome fight that would be? Polar bears can weigh as much as 10 adult men, and walruses can be twice as heavy!

## Human help

The island is named after a Russian explorer named Ferdinand P. Wrangel, who spotted it from his ship back in the 1820s, after being told about it by local people. Today, the only people on Wrangel are a small team of scientists and nature wardens—the huts they live in have spikes on the windows to stop polar bears coming in for food!

## A land of mammoths

If you think polar bears and walruses are impressive animals, just wait until you hear about the creatures that *used* to live here. Scientists think Wrangel was the last place that woolly mammoths lived. After getting cut off from the mainland by rising seawater, a big group of these bulky beasts roamed the island until around 4,000 years ago—that's more than 6,000 years after most of the world's mammoths had disappeared! It's still possible to find their ancient tusks if you search hard.

## Pony power

Assateague is famed for its sturdy, long-maned horses, which roam the woods and marshes in wild herds. They're sometimes known as Chincoteague ponies, even though they live on Assateague and they're horses! Around 300 of them are found here on the island, and many have gorgeous white patches. There have been wild horses on Assateague for hundreds of years, but there are different stories about how they first arrived—one legend is that they're descended from horses that escaped a nearby Spanish shipwreck in the 16th century!

## Take a swim

Every summer, a group of "saltwater cowboys" herd the horses across the sea channel between Assateague and Chincoteague. Seeing hundreds of hooves plunging into the water is a very splashy sight! The horses spend a few days on Chincoteague, where some of the foals are sold to raise money for vet treatments and the local fire service, then they are herded back a couple of days later.

## Lift-off

Keep your eyes on the sky if you visit Chincoteague. A short distance to the south is the wonderfully named Wallops Island—which has a rocket launch site! When a spacecraft takes off, people sometimes crowd onto Chincoteague to watch it zoom above the clouds.

## Twin islands

The twin islands have a lot in common, but they're certainly not identical. Assateague is so long and thin that its top and bottom are in two different states: Maryland and Virginia. Its stretched-out shape also acts as a barrier that shelters the much smaller Chincoteague from the ocean.

# Assateague & Chincoteague Islands
## USA

Lying shoulder to shoulder on the east coast of the USA, Assateague and Chincoteague are sandy islands with a wild side. Ponies canter over the grass, deer browse the trees, and ducks flock together in the bays. Tall forests cluster near the shore and endless pale beaches stretch out for miles, facing the white-tipped waves of the Atlantic Ocean. The views are big, the air is fresh, and the winds are strong.

The horses swim across the channel between islands here.

## Long-standing lighthouse

Like so many islands around the world, Assateague has a lighthouse on its shoreline. Built more than 150 years ago, this red-and-white tower is still going strong, flashing its warning beam at passing ships. The light can be seen more than 18 miles out to sea!

# La Gomera
## Canary Islands

This sun-shaped island is one of Spain's loveliest secrets. The travelers who come here aren't looking for big tourist resorts or beachside discos. Instead, they're coming to enjoy an island full of misty green hills and craggy rocks, a place where the ocean smashes into the cliffs and hiking paths wriggle across the slopes. People have lived here since the Stone Age, which means little La Gomera also has a big history.

Many of the beaches in the Canary Islands have black sand.

### Give a whistle

For thousands of years, the islanders have had an amazing way of communicating across long distances. They whistle messages to each other! Silbo is an ancient language found only on La Gomera. It uses special whistling sounds, all of which mean different things, and the noise can travel for miles across the island's deep valleys. Even today, children at school in La Gomera are taught how to understand Silbo.

### Columbus calling

The island has a special claim to fame. In 1492, the famous explorer Christopher Columbus made a legendary sea voyage from Europe to America—and La Gomera was the place where he made his last stop before crossing the Atlantic. He came here to stock up on food, water, and firewood for the long journey ahead, and he found the island so useful that he came here again, twice.

### Sea life

The seas around the island are rich in marine life. At different times of year, loggerhead turtles, bottlenose dolphins, and pilot whales can all be spotted in the waves. You can even take a special boat trip to see these incredible creatures for yourself.

## In the Canaries
La Gomera is part of Spain's Canary Islands archipelago. Colorful wild canaries still flutter from tree to tree here, but the birds were named after the islands—not the other way around!

## Growing good food
Like many other warm islands, La Gomera produces lots of delicious fruit and vegetables. Many of its hills have flat shelves of land cut into their slopes so that people can plant different crops and trees. The valleys are good for growing dates, avocados, and bananas, and the sunny south of the island is just right for growing grapes, figs, and tomatoes!

### An island called Christmas

The island was given its festive name by a sea captain named Richard Rowe, on Christmas Day in 1643. No one lived here then, but now it's home to people from many different cultures.

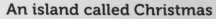

CHRISTMAS
1643

### Crazy creepy-crawlies

Christmas Island has billions of yellow crazy ants, which were first brought here by accident many years ago. Their name might be funny, but the insects themselves are bad news for the island—the ants spray a natural acid to defend themselves, which is very harmful to the island's original inhabitants, red crabs.

# Christmas Island
## Australia

### Top of the mountain

Christmas Island is actually the tip of an enormous mountain, most of which is hidden below the waves. Scientists think it was formed around 66 million years ago.

Don't expect to see Santa Claus sunbathing here! This lush tropical island sits way out in the Indian Ocean, circled by warm blue waters and smothered in humid rainforest. It also has a very special secret: it's the summit of a huge underwater mountain! And although fewer than 2,000 people live here, the island has tens of millions of other residents. Be careful, though—lots of them have very sharp claws ...

Manta rays can often be seen swimming offshore.

## On the march

These scuttling crustaceans are Christmas Island red crabs, a species which is only found in this corner of the world. More than 40 million of them live here on the island, but for most of the year they stay deep in the jungle, sheltering in small burrows.

When the rainy season arrives in October, however, they take a mass journey to the coast to breed. Can you imagine seeing 40 million crabs on the move? This red army swarms across roads, streams, and gardens to reach the seaside—local people have even built special tunnels and bridges to help them!

The red crabs help the rainforest stay healthy by eating fallen leaves, and "plowing" the soil when they make their burrows.

## Bird island

Every year around 80,000 seabirds come here to nest, including the rare Christmas Island frigatebird. Male frigatebirds have an unusual way of attracting females— they can puff out their bright red throats like balloons!

# Where in the World?

**SURTSEY**
Country: Iceland
Size: 1.1 miles long,
0.8 miles wide
Area: 0.54 square miles
Population: 0

**ELLIS ISLAND**
Country: United States
of America
Size: 0.3 miles long,
0.2 miles wide
Area: 0.04 square miles
Population: 0

**ST. KILDA**
Country: United Kingdom
Size: Hilda, the largest island,
is 2.6 miles long,
1.6 miles wide
Area: 3.3 square miles
Population: 0

**ASSATEAGUE AND
CHINCOTEAGUE ISLANDS**
Country: United States of America
Size: Assateague: 37 miles long,
1.6 miles wide;
Chincoteague: 8.1 miles long,
2 miles wide
Area: Assateague: 24.3 square miles;
Chincoteague: 9.1 square miles
Population: Chincoteague: 2,899;
Assateague: 0

**PITCAIRN ISLAND**
Country: Pitcairn Islands
Size: 2 miles long,
1 mile wide
Area: 1.9 square miles
Population: 55

**LA GOMERA**
Country: Spain
Size: 16 miles long,
16 miles wide
Area: 378 square miles
Population: 21,503

**EASTER ISLAND**
Country: Chile
Size: 14.3 miles long,
7 miles wide
Area: 63 square miles
Population: 7,750

**GALÁPAGOS ISLANDS**
Country: Ecuador
Size: 13 larger islands and 7 smaller
islands. The largest island, Isabela, is
75 miles long and
43.5 miles wide.
Total Land Area: 3,090
square miles
Population: 25,124

**UROS FLOATING
ISLANDS**
Country: Peru
Size: Approximately 120
floating islands, each about
0.06 to 0.12 miles long
Population: 1,200

**SNOW HILL ISLAND**
Continent: Antarctica
Size: 25 miles long,
7.5 miles wide
Area: 143 square miles
Population: 0

**ÎLE DE LA CITÉ**
**Country:** France
**Size:** 0.75 miles long,
0.2 miles wide
**Area:** 0.08 square miles
**Population:** 981

**SANTORINI**
**Country:** Greece
**Size:** 11.2 miles long,
7.5 miles wide
**Area:** 28 square miles
**Population:** 15,550

**WRANGEL ISLAND**
**Country:** Russia
**Size:** 50 miles long,
78 miles wide
**Area:** 2937 square miles
**Population:** 0

**MIYAJIMA**
**Country:** Japan
**Size:** 5.6 miles long,
3.7 miles wide
**Area:** 12 square miles
**Population:** 2,000

**CHRISTMAS ISLAND**
**Country:** Australia
**Size:** 11.8 miles long,
9 miles wide
**Area:** 52 square miles
**Population:** 1,843

**FRASER ISLAND**
**Country:** Australia
**Size:** 76 miles long,
13.7 miles wide
**Area:** 702 square miles
**Population:** 182

**SOCOTRA**
**Country:** Yemen
**Size:** 84 miles long,
20.5 miles wide
**Area:** 1,400 square miles
**Population:** 44,000

**PALM JUMEIRAH**
**Country:** United Arab Emirates
**Size:** 3 miles long,
3.3 miles wide
**Area:** 2.2 square miles
**Population:** 10,500

47

# Ten Other Islands to Explore

If you've been inspired by reading about all the fascinating islands in this book, here are some more that you might want to research and explore.

## Mont-Saint-Michel, France

This is a famous tidal island topped by the spire of a 500-year-old abbey.

## Culebra, Puerto Rico

This was once a naval base, but now it is a center for wildlife, beaches, and snorkeling.

## Si Phan Don, Laos

These tropical sandy islands are on the River Mekong, far from any ocean.

## Barro Colorado, Panama

This island nature reserve in a lake is home to hundreds of plant and animal species.

## Skellig Michael, Ireland

Scenes from Star Wars were filmed here among jagged green cliffs.

## Silhouette Island, the Seychelles

This idyllic island is home to sea turtles, kestrels, fruit bats, land tortoises, and much more.

## Robben Island, South Africa

The great political leader Nelson Mandela survived 18 years in prison here.

## Ap Lei Chau, Hong Kong

You cross a bridge to reach this tiny city island with more than 85,000 residents.

## Rügen, Germany

This is an island famous for its long sandy beaches, tall forests, and chalk cliffs.

## Udo, Korea

The name of this green rocky island means "cow"—because it's shaped like one.